# COMMON SENSE

## 1996

this time it's a no brainer

# COMMON SENSE

# 1996

## this time it's a no brainer

By Thomas Pain

First Edition

Published by:
The Institute for American Liberty Press, formerly
The Institute for American Democracy Press,
a division of
HEARTLAND COMMUNICATIONS CORPORATION

Editor: Mark Draper, PhD

RAW PUBLICATIONS LLC
1320 Old Chain Bridge Road
Suite 220
McLean, Virginia 22101
703–883–1355

# DEDICATION

To Robert and Loy LeFevre,
who taught and inspired me
and to all the Little Guys of the World

LET THERE BE PEACE ON EARTH
AND LET IT BEGIN WITH ME

# TABLE OF CONTENTS

# FOREWORD

In 1776, Thomas Paine wrote:

*These are the times that try men's souls. The summer soldier and the sunshine patriot will, in this crises, shrink from the service of his country; but he that stands it now deserves the love and thanks of man and women. Tyranny, like Hell, is not easily conquered; yet we have this consolation with us, that the harder the conflict, the more glorious the triumph.*

Now, over two hundred years later, these words still inspire. But too many of us have become confused. Tyranny has not been conquered. The government of the United States has gradually become more paternalistic, more expensive and more intrusive than the British Empire which inspired the revolt of 1776. Now, the need for some common sense is greater than ever before.

Unfortunately, Tom Paine died more than one hundred eighty six years ago. And, no modern day thinker, statesman or even a politician appears able to fill the void left by his passing. Even the "revolutionaries" elected in 1994 are incapable of doing more than merely paying lip service to the ideals of Tom Paine.

It was Tom Paine who first advocated term limits over two hundred years ago when the Constitution was being written. And, events have proven that Tom Paine and his contemporaries had good reason to view government with suspicion, as a dangerous device to be limited. Consider the following:

The Constitution of the United States forbids a direct tax. It was only by an ill-advised constitutional amendment early in this century that the income tax came into existence.

The revolutionaries of 1776 never contemplated a national paramilitary police force such as has been created by the FBI, DEA and BATF, which routinely violates the liberty of American citizens.

The ability of government agents to seize property through forfeiture and the procedure by which taxing authorities and other regulators routinely force individuals to prove their innocence are perversions of the intent of the authors of the Constitution and the Bill of Rights worthy of the Third Reich, or the Soviet State, not the United States.

The welfare state, which presumes that government is better able than the individual to make decisions that impact his or her life, is another modern invention.

Other examples of the error of our ways can be found in these items:
- a monetary system based upon good PR;
- persistent foreign adventurism;
- something we call "free trade" but which is really a program of import and export subsidies granted by bureaucrats to those with influence; and,
- a bloated government payroll with over 800,000 non-essential employees. If they aren't essential why were they hired in the first place?

Americans have become what Tom Paine would have called indentured servants for at least 128 days a year just to pay their ever-growing tax bills. Indentured servitude really isn't sufficient to convey the horror of our predicament as we struggle to pay the public and private debt which must accumulate in any system relying upon debt based money as a medium of exchange.

Debt piles upon debt. Remember the "miracle of compound interest" you learned about in school.

As interest costs climb, the prices of raw materials and labor and the profits of private enterprise must fall in order to pay the interest. This makes us believe "cheaper is better." Therefore, we scour the world looking for the cheapest food, fuel, minerals, building materials and labor. Over the past twenty years real wages have steadily declined. Between 1989 and 1992 the profits of private enterprise were as low (as a percentage of National Income) as during the depths of the Great Depression.

As our wages and profits decline in real terms, we borrow more and more to sustain our lifestyles. As our wages and profits decline in real terms so do government tax receipts.

But the artificial demand for social welfare spending, created by politicians seeking to buy votes, increases as more and more Americans receive subsidies to survive. Government borrows to keep making the transfer payments received by more than 50% of Americans. Pity the poor politician who attempts to curb these entitlements! Taxes go up, in real terms, to pay the interest on the federal debt and finance the ever-growing government.

Under the twin economic pressures of higher debt service and taxes, social mores begin to break down. People look for the quick fix, the big score. Those who work for a living at the minimum wage aren't making enough to survive and are considered "chumps" by those who operate outside of the law and "take" for a living.

Why go to school when there are only "McJobs" to look forward to?

Why work for a living and raise a family?

No, the answer is live for today. Get it while you can.

Eventually, the standards of the street fall to the lowest common denominator: survival. The end justifies the means, the means become the end and there is no regard for the common good. This morality of the street is the same whether the location is Wall Street, Pennsylvania Avenue or the "Mean" Street in your town. The only difference is whether the predators use guns or pens to take what they want.

The situation is making it impossible to sustain our communities and families in a society corrupted by the over concentration of political and economic power in too few hands. Today, common sense is in short supply.

Clearly, these are the "times that try men's souls." What are we to do? We refuse to be sunshine patriots. We refuse to resort to futile violence. Our first effort is aimed at helping to end the confusion. That's why we started *America the Beautiful,* a nationally syndicated radio program where we talk about, "the people and ideas that make this country great, free market solutions to the problems that threaten that greatness and how one person can make a difference and you can be that person!"

Being in radio means all things are possible. If America needs more common sense, we refuse to let a little thing like mortality stand in the way of giving America that common sense. So, one hundred eighty six plus years after his death, *America the Beautiful* simply resurrected Tom Pain.

Each Wednesday afternoon we introduce Tom Pain as our favorite dead man and he makes a cameo appearance to share some common sense. As you might have guessed, the reappearance of Tom Pain after a one hundred eighty six year hiatus created something of a sensation among our listeners.

In fact the reaction has been so good Tom has agreed to get back into the publishing business and this book represents the assembled common sense heard over the past year on *America The Beautiful.*

For a dead man, Tom Pain does a really good job of keeping his finger on the pulse of modern politics. Tom Pain has an uncanny ability to cut through the smoke, mirrors and spin which living politicians use to confuse voters and taxpayers. After all these years underground Tom Pain hasn't got the patience to waste time and energy on silly things like who sits where on Air Force One or whether a reduction in the rate at which government spending grows is a cut or not. Tom Pain doesn't waste time and energy on how the President's wife does her hair this week or what she was or wasn't called by the Mother of the Speaker of the House.

Instead, Tom Pain get's down to the basic issues confronting each of us as citizens and taxpayers. What is government? What should government do? What can government do? How should government be paid for? And, most importantly, what each of us can do to take control of our own destiny and put an end to the monkey business that threatens to undo the good Tom and his friends did the last time around. So, read on. If you missed Tom Pain on *America The Beautiful,* here is your chance to catch up. Here is a good solid dose of *Common Sense 1996* from Tom Pain.

Michael Foudy
McLean, Virginia
December 12, 1995

# PREFACE

Made up of essays I delivered on the radio program, *Mike Foudy's America the Beautiful*, this little book, a short course in the essentials of American liberty has two prerequisites. First, to appreciate this book fully, you need to be able to think. Given the massive failure of statist schools, this is a requirement that will be more honored in breach than in practice. Like *The Federalist Papers*, the original edition of *Common Sense* was written for the man in the street. But many college graduates of today would find such demanding prose beyond their reach.

Second, it requires intellectual courage, a willingness to recognize that much of what you have been taught and conditioned to think about your government is false. You will find much of your thinking challenged by this work. You will read that there exist better solutions to social problems than merely relying on the machinery of the centralized federal government. You may conclude that such machinery is dangerous and demonstrably obsolete.

I ask you to open your mind, ponder the conditioning process you have been through—and which you experience in the media each day. Allow your mind to examine thoroughly the ideas presented here. Read the entire book before reaching your conclusions. Think them through, putting aside all dogma, and you will discover much truth and no little common sense.

# INTRODUCTION

I would remain in the grave's embrace, but my spirit, hearing the cadence of drums, the pealing of bells, answers my country's call to action. Rising, I find a nation confused and ignorant of the meaning of the Spirit of '76. America must hear once more the ideals which gave her birth in the American Revolution of 1776 and which shall give her new life in her current trials.

The people must wake from their deep slumber. The hour is at hand to preserve our country and with it, all hope of liberty for men throughout the world bowed beneath the chains of tyranny.

But this reawakened truth will not be universally welcomed. The truth so disturbs small men that they shout it down rather than face its troubling implications. They wish rather to stay in a stupor as the media reassuringly washes over them each day.

Regardless of their flight from reality, I shall speak here once more the unvarnished common sense, truth without compromise.

These timeless ideas may strike the uneducated ear as foreign. Ignorant of the true meaning of the first American Revolution, they will not recognize their own birthright in its native land. The meaning of that revolution centered on *individual freedom*. It was about the *individual* breaking free from government regulations and suppression.

The first American Revolution was based on principles of human action that are demonstrably true and self-evident. The value of these ideals has been proven by the experience of human history, especially the incredible success of the American experiment. Centering around the principle that the more liberty, the more prosperity, these ideals gave birth to the mightiest nation on earth, an incredible country whose amazing prosperity results from and is matched by previously unimagined political freedoms.

We begin our intellectual journey with definitions, a statement of principles, then essays which apply the preceding.

May this journey start you on the road to an expanded awareness of your full rights as a human being. May you learn to respect the boundaries of others as you require the regard of others for your own boundaries. I trust you will learn the morality of voluntary action and the immorality of force and coercion.

One important principle you will explore here is the cost/benefit analysis or balancing test. Each time someone argues that another government program is desperately needed, you should immediately ask if there are alternative ways of approaching the problem. Always keep in mind that it is an imperfect world and always will be so. The politician, intent on preserving his power and perks will tell you that only he can solve this nation's problems, but he is this nation's problem.

Then you apply the cost/benefit analysis. For example: Is it worth it to tax and impoverish everyone in order to fight poverty? Or, are we better off leaving money in the hands of those who earn it? Both morally and practically, we are better off with the money in your hands. Not only is the laborer worthy of his hire, but he knows best what represents the best use of his own earnings.

You will hear the hue and cry that society will deteriorate if we don't have a governmental safety net. But decades of ever-growing government programs and meddling into our affairs has bankrupted us financially and morally. The results speak for themselves. The safety net has become an enmeshing snare. We have become prisoners of the mindless bureaucrats who have fattened on the waste of well-intentioned government programs.

History shows that when government comes in, common sense departs. All problems are worsened and everyone is thereby impoverished.

If we create a government to protect our property which then regularly steals away up to half of it each year through taxes, how in the world are we better off? Should we not rather keep our money and solve our own problems?

To answer such questions, we must apply the balancing test: If an idea is great and a real problem is there to be solved, what is the best way to deal with it? Should there be more government programs or should money be left in private hands to find free and voluntary solutions?

Most reasonable people agree on goals. Everyone wants prosperity and not poverty. We hate crime and violence and want to be able to walk our streets in safety. We want strong families, good schools, equality before the law, a maximum of personal freedom. We all know what America should be. Where the disagreement comes is in how best to deal with our problems and create the society for which we all yearn.

Of course, there are those who resist change. The ruling elite warn that chaos will reign should we truly strive to achieve America's true destiny. Yet, this elite has created utter chaos with their obsolete governmental methodology. A nation founded on theft (tax), creating valueless people through a collectivist approach to problems is dragging us all down.

Here is the crux of the problem: In the pleasant living of the 1950s, a family of 4 could live well on one 40-hour workweek. Now, the same family has to work 80 hours per week just to get by. This is primarily due to taxes to pay for every wonderful-sounding scheme on earth. In the '50s, we worked till mid-February to pay taxes. Now, we work till mid-May.

In the 1950s, a family of four headed by an average blue collar worker paid about 2% income tax. Today, that same worker's tax burden has increased 15 fold. The middle class stiff is getting his cojones busted by a bloated bunch of bureaucrats who will get off neither their butts nor his back. We now have more civil servants shuffling paper than we have real people with real jobs manufacturing something that makes life better for people.

Joe Sixpack, the guy who makes this country work, is carrying 15 times his fair share of the load to support a bunch of guys who have never had a real job, who make no useful products, who provide no needful services but merely suck up an unfair share of the goodies for doing nothing but making life miserable for Joe and his family.

Americans like Joe all across our country are working harder and bringing home less, fighting an economic battle for their families and their future. We used to have the highest wages in the world. Now, a dozen other countries pay higher wages. Thanks to an investment capital base devastated by excessive taxes, productivity growth rates are falling. For too many Americans, the average work week is longer than it was 20 years ago, but real wages are lower than they were 10 years ago. Taxes are bleeding us dry, sapping our family budgets and draining the nation's economic strength. The growing deficit caused by wasteful programs is ruining our economy. The debt and interest payments now consume nearly 20 cents of every American tax dollar.

These taxes and government regulation are also destroying our middle class, the traditional safeguard of traditional values. We must drastically slash government in order to restore the good life for the average family. Slashing government is for the little guy, not the big guy. If you taxed away 100% of the annual income from the rich, it would pay for government for 3 weeks. The money comes from the little guy despite the constant lie you are told. Also, if corporate taxes are raised, the cost is always passed along to you. People don't work for nothing.

Fundamentally, the issues boil down to the statists (socialists) versus free market people. No matter what the problem, to the statists the solution is always government. Free market people favor money in private hands. The politicians are all statists. The Republicans and the Democrats are the *Republicrats*. There isn't a dime's worth of difference between them despite all the hot air and the media saying that they are far apart, etc. They aren't far apart as they represent the governmental machinery in place. Using the scale of one million dollars being equal to one inch, the 1.5 trillion dollar budget being so hotly debated equals 25 miles. The difference between the Republicans and Clinton is 25 FEET! or .00011%. Left wing, right wing, same dirty bird.

The Republicans are trumpeting the virtues of their new budget which, they claim, will balance in 7 years. If you believe that, the Tooth Fairy will be coming to your house soon. Evidently you are part of the hold-over group who believed all those promises that the income tax would never go over 2% when enacted. An example of what the Republicans have done—advertised as "decreasing the rate of increase of programs" is Head Start. This program, demonstrated to make no permanent gains in learning ability, has had its budget double over the last three years. The Republicans want to cut it by 4%. You would think that children were being boiled in oil from the outcry. Folks, a 4% reduction does not begin to address our problem and neither does a slower growth budget. We need to slash this government by 75% and leave your income tax dollars in your hands. That is a real revolution, not a bogus "Republican Revolution" which turns out to be nothing but more of the same minus 4%.

One of the tragic effects of the PR for the Republican statists is that they have become identified with the free market. Therefore, when their programs fail, as they inevitably will, the blame will be placed on the free market. Remember, their programs are the continuation of the same statist approach. They argue over freckles on the body politic, not elimination of the statist approach.

They will ask you "O.K., what is your solution to the problem?" Well, there is no perfect solution, unlike what they promise. The market is the most effective, most moral and cheapest way to attack a problem. Solution number one is for the ruling elite to get off our backs with their compulsory taxation and coercive statist methodology.

What if you got to keep all you earned? Just imagine yourself with all of your income tax in your pocket. The statists argue that no one would help the little guy without government coercion. How could we possibly know, since they steal so much of our money? We don't have the luxury of being charitable. Government programs have eroded the opportunity for private charity.

To those who say that voluntary organizations would never be created to address the problems of the little guy, I say you are ignorant of history and the American spirit. As for history, no vast welfare system existed during the Great Depression; instead families and neighbors drew together and helped one another survive the economic hard times brought on by and exacerbated by government interference with the free market.

As for the unique can-do American spirit, a century and a half ago Alexis de Tocqueville observed that, whereas Europeans looked to central governments to accomplish tasks, Americans were self-reliant, working side by side with neighbors to achieve common goals.

Those who think that spirit is dead need to read the report released this summer by Volunteer Centre U.K., Britain's leading charitable clearinghouse. This survey of nine European nations found that 27% of their citizens had done some volunteer work this year. In contrast, nearly half (48%) of Americans volunteer regularly, serving nearly 20 billion hours last year. If the government would simply get out of their way, Americans' willingness to serve would soar even higher.

But our so-called leaders, Gingrich, Dole, Clinton *et al.* simply want power over us, and the little guy is their excuse. They simply trade places as the spokespersons for large government, statist methodology and they convince you that you control them because you get to select (vote) who will be in charge of this monstrous machinery every few years.

That's a little bit like being a galley slave who gets to select the captain of the ship every four years. The ship remains the same. So do the whippings.

I hope you will read through the materials that follow with an open mind. Many people who came before gave us the gift of liberty. It's time to spread the understanding of that message.

# GLOSSARY OF TERMS

GENERAL WELFARE:  I never met him. Before he came here he was a Kernel in the Red Army.

STATIST:  Those who seek to solve problems by governmental or socialistic methods.

DEMOCRAT:  Statist.

REPUBLICAN:  Statist.

INDEPENDENT:  Statist.

LIBERAL:  Statist.

CONSERVATIVE:  Statist.

REPUBLICRAT:  Statist.

BUREAUCRAT:  Statist.

RUSH LIMBAUGH:  A statist-socialist wrapped deceptively in occasional free-market rhetoric. A tonic for the unwary. An apologist for the establishment masked as a foe of the establishment.

THEFT:  The seizing and carrying away of property without consent of the owner.

POLITICIAN:  Thief, nice person typically, but a thief just the same.

BUREAUCRAT:  See definition for "politician."

ROBB AND DOLE:  Daily government activity—most accurate political names of all time.

DEMOCRATIC HOUSE MEMBER OR SENATOR:  Those who say they are trying to help the poor and disadvantaged while actually maintaining the special interests and lining their own pockets.

REPUBLICAN HOUSE MEMBER OR SENATOR:  Those who say they are trying to help the small business owner while actually maintaining the special interests and lining their own pockets.

LITTLE GUY:  Anyone, male or female, striving for a place in the sun.

INTERSTATE COMMERCE:  Anything the courts want it to be.

INDIVIDUAL:  The primary unit of society.

MILITARY INTELLIGENCE:  Like Postal Service and Congressional Ethics, an oxymoron.

JAIL INDUSTRIAL COMPLEX:  The tragic condition of U.S. society.

FIJA:  Fully Informed Jury Association.

JURY:  People who decide the facts and the merit of the law.

MONOPOLY:  Economic disaster sustained over long periods only by government interference.

GOVERNMENT CORRUPTION:  Yes.

CENTRAL PLANNING:  Universal disaster.

VIETNAM WAR:  The direct result of centralized power and planning—two million people died.

ELECTION:  Advance auction of stolen goods.

REGULATION:  Strangulation.

RULING ELITE:  Endangered species.

GOVERNMENT:  (1) The cause of virtually all social problems, (2) an obsolete methodology.

GOVERNMENT HELP:  An oxymoronic term for the plague.

FREEDOM:  The solution to virtually all social problems.

THE FREE MARKET:  Although imperfect, the best, most efficient and most moral way to solve human problems.

GOVERNMENT SOLUTIONS:  The most imperfect, immoral and counter-productive method of approaching problems.

MAFIA:  A shadow government with a vastly more efficient and cost-effective justice system.

GOVERNMENT PROGRAM:  A solution worse than the problem.

GOVERNMENT REGULATION:  (1) Protection for Big Business, (2) The dumbing down of consumers at monopolistic prices.

PUBLIC SERVICE:  Self-service for the ruling elite.

SELF-INTEREST:  The mainspring of all human action.

STAR SPANGLED BANNER:  A war and killing song adopted as the national anthem in 1935 to prepare us for bloodshed.

AMERICA THE BEAUTIFUL:  The real song of America.

UNCLE SAM:  Not my uncle, not even my friend. A clever, slick public relations symbol masking evil. Certainly not uncle sugar.

GOOD GOVERNMENT:  An oxymoron.

GOVERNMENT:  A tool to benefit some by injuring others.

PRIVATE PROPERTY:  The essential element of civilized society.

PROPERTY:  Not just real estate. Yourself and the fruits of your labor.

SPIRITUALITY:  A necessary ingredient in life.

RELIGION:  Strictly personal.

WAR:  The normal condition of the State.

THE DRAFT:  Slavery in the name of freedom.

CHARITY:  The natural inclination of man when his resources are not stolen.

FAMILY:  The joyful foundation of the good life, second only to the primacy of the individual.

GOVERNMENTS:  Force and evil wrapped in hype and public relations.

RACISM:  Ignorant absurdity.

CIVIL SOCIETY:  Characterized by voluntarism and peaceful exchange.

PUBLIC SCHOOLS:  Government schools—as anticipated—an unmitigated disaster; teaching our kids to become compliant, obedient little soldiers.

GOVERNMENT PLANNING:  The formulation by the unwise for exploitation of the unwary.

TAX:  Theft.

ESTATE TAX:  Double theft.

RULING ELITE:  Those who will soon be looking for real jobs.

STATE DEPARTMENT:  An organized meddling methodology to get us into trouble.

GOOD:  There is no limit to the good do-gooders will do with other peoples money.

COLIN POWELL AND OTHERS ASPIRING TO THE PRESI-DENCY:  Very nice people, possible successors as Captains of the *Titanic.* Possible new public relations representatives of our monstrous federal government.

PRESIDENTIAL ELECTION:  Illusory charade that makes people think they are changing things when they basically stay the same.

REPUBLICAN REVOLUTION:  Business as usual, the status quo wrapped in hype and disinformation.

REPUBLICAN REVOLUTION:  Bullshit in a teapot.

CONSERVATIVE REVOLUTION:  An oxymoron.

MEDIA:  Public relations service for government methodology (socialism—statism), purveyors of hype and confusion, prostitutes of persuasion.

INSANITY:  Doing the same thing over and over again and expecting the results to be different.

REVOLUTION:  Not an illusory change in managers of a monster—a complete change in methodology.

THE PEN:  Mightier than the sword.

POWER:  Nothing is so powerful as an idea whose time has come.

# CHAPTER 1

# SOME BASIC PRINCIPLES

1.   "The significant problems we have cannot be solved at the same level of thinking with which we created them."—Albert Einstein.

2.   Government does not work, despite lofty and laudable objectives.

3.   Most people in government mean to do well. They are in a system where they have never questioned the morality or effectiveness of the entire approach. Therefore, nothing herein should be taken personally by anyone. The purpose is to find solutions to problems and individuals have nothing to do with basic criticisms. The system is what doesn't work.

4.   Violence is totally wrong, abhorrent and counter-productive.

5.   Government is violence and force.

6.   Government must be vastly reduced; individuals will thrive and prosper in direct relation to this reduction. Reduced taxes = accumulated capital = investment = jobs. This is not trickle down. It's the middle class who invest the most.

7.   The free market is the best way to solve problems . . . and the most moral.

8.   What is done is done. In terms of the future, the relevant question is where do we go from here? Forget who struck John.

We should not linger over wars that should not have been fought, legislation that should not have been passed, unions that were busted or given too much governmental power. History is history and its only use is for purposes of instruction so we don't repeat it. In other words, the criticisms of historical actions are only made with an idea to shape future problem-solving so we won't repeat our mistakes.

9.    Individuals should not take any of this personally. A person cannot help it if he is inadvertently involved in theft because of obfuscation.

10.    I am very aware that there have been and are a number of highly talented individuals with great integrity and lofty purpose who have served and are serving in government, both in political office and in the bureaucracy. However, these individuals have been swept away in a monstrous system. Their integrity and statesmanship have been overwhelmed by coercion and force and the cancerous growth of government. Therefore I use direct and sometimes harsh language to snap folks back to reality and to get the hype and mysticism out of the overriding travesty that is occurring. To those people who have tried and are trying to bring sanity into the system I say thanks, but you have failed and will continue to fail in the absence of true dramatic and revolutionary change.

11.    Do not fear the consequences of changing the methodology of solving problems and reducing government. Have confidence in the undeniable fact that the fewer taxes and the less government interference, the more prosperity and progress for everyone.

12.    "You cannot by reasoning correct a man of ill opinion which by reasoning he never acquired."—Bacon.

# CHAPTER 2

# WHERE AM I COMING FROM?

As you are aware I am Thomas Pain or Tom Pain, if you prefer. Remember me? If so, you must have studied American history before it was rewritten by the PC Brigade. A generation ago, every schoolchild recognized my name as that of someone instrumental in the American Revolution of 1776 when we broke from Great Britain. My book *Common Sense* was the first to argue to Americans that we must break from Great Britain.

Recall also that I published under the name of Publius, because I was afraid the Crown would hang me for treason.

Really, I was hoping that I would not have to come back. But, as you know things are a real mess. We all love our country, but our government stinks.

Most of the things that we worried might go wrong, have gone wrong. Back when I first wrote, we fought the revolutionary war over a simple, silly little single tax called a stamp tax.

How many taxes are there today? Thousands and not just at the federal level.

Incidentally, I have dropped the "e" from Paine this time . . . my last name is spelled PAIN because we are all in such pain from our out-of-control government.

I have come back to set the record straight and to talk about common sense again because there is so much baloney and dou-ble-speak being perpetuated by the government and media today in these United States of America. Double speak example: a tax loophole is where you get to keep your own money.

Let's talk some basic philosophy and truth. In the 1700s, we knew—and you need to be reminded—that tax is theft. Theft is defined as the taking of the property from another without their consent. Have you consented to all the taxes you pay? I don't think so. Would you like a chance to vote on a few specific taxes so they could be repealed?

ONCE AGAIN, WRITE THIS DOWN:  TAX IS THEFT. That is why we put into the Constitution that there would be no income tax. After being reassured endlessly by the ruling elite that the income tax would never go above 1% or 2%, Americans repealed the Constitutional prohibition of an income tax in 1913.

For most of our nation's 220-year history, we managed without an income tax. Can you imagine what you could do with your money if you did not pay income tax?

WHY IS TAX THEFT? Here is an illustration. If you and two friends were on a desert island and voted 2 to 1 to kill one of the others, that would be murder. The vote does not and cannot make an immoral act moral. If you voted 2 to 1 to steal the property of the other, that is a wrong and an immoral act. It is not moral to violate the boundaries of another without the consent of that person.

Just because we organize a group to violate the boundaries of another does not make the act moral. When is it moral for the group to do that which is not moral for an individual to do? Never!

How can you have a moral society that is founded on theft? The methodology of how many tasks are accomplished today is by tax or theft. Taxes are running wild at every level.

You have been conned by the politicians and the media. They tell you that they are after the rich. If you taxed all the annual income of the rich it would pay for the federal government for 3 weeks. The income tax falls on the middle class because that's where the money is. The politicians lie to you and tell you that they are taxing the big guy . . . the fact is you pay for what they are doing. The big guy doesn't have enough.

They also seek to frighten you and tell you that you will lose school lunches or Medicare. Imagine if the income tax were abolished and you had all of your earned income in your pocket. Could you pay for school lunches? Could you buy health insurance?

We should search for the truth in our lives, no matter how unpleasant. Common sense tells us that the politicians and our government have lied to us. They produce nothing, they must take from the little guy, only to give some money back after huge service charges.

And what do they do with the money? For the most part, what the government does best is MANUFACTURE VALUELESS PEOPLE.

Between welfare and absurd drug laws, the government has created a threatening place.

In the 1950s, a man with a high school diploma could give a family of four a good life on a 40-hour work week, now it takes 80 hours. This is mostly due to taxes at every level. When Clinton talks about hardship on the average person, he fails to mention that the reason for this hardship is expropriative taxes.

We do not need a giant nanny. We can manage our own lives. Tax is theft, and it's time for the repeal of the income tax.

Remember that the revolution of 1776 was fought over one simple tax. We need to repeal the income tax for starters. You can do two things right now to help save America and yourself from these tax burdens. One is to join the American Initiative Committee (to bypass Congress), 800–307–8425. Second, pay attention to libertarian candidates. They want to abolish the income tax and cut the Federal Government by 2/3.

Also, always remember that violence and force beget violence and force. The government *is* organized violence and force. We must go forth for peaceful change. I hope you adopt what I have adopted. I promise not to violate your boundaries. Let there be peace on earth and let it begin with me.

# CHAPTER 3

# LIFE, LIBERTY, AND PROPERTY

When the Declaration of Independence was first drafted, the words said: "We hold these truths to be self-evident, that we are endowed by our creator with life, liberty and property." The word property was changed to "pursuit of happiness."

It's too bad the words were changed. Property is a more important and profound concept. In fact, property and the recognition of private property is the primary reason why our nation has been so much more prosperous than others. More than any other nation, we dared to allow the individual to retain the fruits of his labor. The result has been the creation of wealth on a scale unmatched in history.

What is a self-evident truth? It is one that is true for the human species in the context of our life on earth. Certain principles and truths have been discovered, but mankind has remained ignorant of them until recently. Truths are now sweeping the world.

Most truths of human relationships that are sweeping the world have to do with the clear demonstration of the superiority of the free market over centralized planned economies.

What does this have to do with property? First of all, you have a right to your life as it says in the Declaration of Independence, you have a right to liberty and in order to live your life and in order to sustain life and liberty you need property.

Your self is your first property. As long as you are alive, you will never be broke because you own a major asset . . . yourself! Each person has boundaries around himself. I do not have a right to violate your boundary by striking or injuring you or by taking your property.

When a group combines to steal the property of another (taxation) it is a fundamental infraction of a natural law or truth which involves the violation of another's boundary.

When the do-gooders decide that some big social problem needs to be addressed, they inevitably want to solve the problem with someone else's money. By stealing money from others (taxation) they create a system in which human boundaries are violated en masse everyday. This has a tendency to create a violent and ugly society in which the most creative and productive members of society are systematically discouraged from making the innovations which enrich us all.

If someone set out to design a system to emasculate the American working class male, to discourage marriage, to develop a permanent underclass, to create a dynasty of welfare dependency, to foster illegitimacy, to punish initiative, to destroy motivation, to breed criminals, to develop drug addicts and alcoholics, they could not come up with anything better adapted to ruining families than our system of welfare.

We are spending the vast resources of our nation to destroy the lives of our citizens. We have spent more losing the war on poverty than we spent winning World War II. We have blown off over 5 trillion dollars on welfare since LBJ launched his war on poverty. That unimaginably huge sum is enough money to transform every one of our inner cities into gleaming paradises. Have you been to Harlem or Detroit or South Central LA lately? With thousands of billions of dollars poured in there, they must be gloriously beautiful havens of culture, right?

LBJ called this massive government spending a great investment. Well, your family and my family and every other American family have each "invested" some $50,000 in this war.

What are the results? The poor are worse off and the inner city looks like a battlezone, the aftermath of a 30-year war.

We should solve our problems through voluntary exchange and association. If you want to direct your funds to save the spotted owl, you should be able to. But if you had the wisdom of an owl, you would not seek to force me to do so.

When we erect the machinery of government to solve problems, we create a permanent boundary-violator. This year, we may be very pleased that our boundary-violator is fighting poverty. But next year, because we have created an agency of force to solve problems, that agency turns on us and fights a war in far-off lands where we have no interest.

What we must do is take the power away from this central boundary violator. Despite its lofty sounding objectives, its activities create the greater harm by injuring everyone (taxing everyone) and violating natural rights (boundary violations) and creating machinery which can be taken over by a man like Hitler who because of majority vote, has the right to inflict his policies.

It is time to dismantle the primary agency of force and injury in the world, our monstrous government.

# CHAPTER 4

# PRODUCERS OF THE WORLD UNITE

You have nothing to lose but your chains, and you have a world to win.

You producers out there know who you are. You are the hard workers who make it possible for the politicians and bureaucrats to have an income through the money they steal from you. A producer is someone who does not live on money stolen from someone else.

If you receive any money from taxes, you are not a producer to that extent. Remember, I told you earlier that tax is theft.

If any of you are living from tax money, please examine the morality of it. If you are on Social Security and don't need it, don't take it. You have already received much more than you paid in. For those that need it, keep it because the system can be fixed without hurting those who need. We need to privatize Social Security, but that's a later subject.

Most people who are in the public trough have elaborate justifications for what they are doing and truly believe that what they are doing is useful. Some, very few, functions of government have some use. We could cut the Federal Government by two-thirds (a good start) and no essential functions would be eliminated. The free market can provide anything that would be missing.

The usual bottom line justification for drawing a government check (apart from social security) is "Well, if I don't take it someone else will." Others truly believe they are superior and are the essential ruling class.

Well, this ruling class is making a mess out of our wonderful country. They are taxing away our integrity, our wealth and they are enslaving us at the same time.

Inside the beltway in Washington, the name of the game is brokering power and money. In 1995 an article appeared in the *Washington Post* pointing out that Webster Hubbell was recently hired by the city of Los Angeles to lobby the Clinton Administration while he was facing fraud charges. Hubbell was paid $25,000 to lobby the Department of Transportation for the L.A. Airport. When Senators leave office, their incomes typically go from $125,000 to $600,000, because they are paid to influence the system.

The system is killing us. Despite all of the lofty objectives such as fighting crime, fighting drugs, and fighting poverty, the financing of the system itself through theft (taxing) our money is impoverishing us all and enriching an elite ruling class. When you have been voting for President, you have been merely changing the quarterback . . . it is a con game to make you think there are big differences between Presidents . . . they differ only in very small degree. They all agree to keep you enslaved and take your money.

Sorry folks, it's the Republicans, Democrats and the Bureaucrats against the people.

It's time for the producers to throw off their chains. If you draw government money, you are part of the problem. All politics are personal. Control yourself and act like a human being and do not be part of the problem. If you wonder what you can do to straighten out the mess in Washington, start with yourself to make sure you are not part of the problem. If you are a producer, you are doing great deal to help this country. You can be proud of yourself. You have done more for your fellow man than any politician ever will.

You see, the rub is the more they try to help us, the more they hurt us. Just as bad for our families as his ripping us off is Uncle Sam's unwanted help. In one area after another, functions once performed by the family have been taken over by the government or bureaucracies and institutions. The government does more and more, and families less and less.

Right now, there are nearly three hundred programs administered by two dozen agencies of the Federal Government whose primary missions are to benefit children and adolescents, recreation programs, drug and alcohol rehabilitation, job training, delinquency prevention, juvenile justice services, nutrition guidance, and so on. Like all social-welfare expenditures, youth program cost has increased ten-fold in the past two decades.

How did this investment increase the well-being of our children? Among white teenagers, suicide has increased 140% since the '60s; homicide, 300% and Gonorrhea up 200%. Among children aged 12 to 17 alcohol use has doubled, and those using drugs up 150%. In the same period, the arrest rate for violent crimes nearly doubled in that age group.

This is the glorious future we have bought with our "investment" in the war on poverty.

We need to destroy these institutions and restore to the family its proper functions. Uncle Sam, leave us alone! We'd rather do it ourselves.

The family fulfills many functions—social, psychological, and even economic—but these are not its purpose.

The purpose of the family is to raise children. We need to give the family a break. The best thing the United States government can do for families is to leave them alone. We don't need a hand out. We don't even need a hand. We simply need Uncle Sam's hand out of our pockets. We don't need the government to solve our problems. The government is the problem. Don't help us. Just quit your systematic attack on the roots of American greatness. Respect the individualism and free markets that create a prosperity unmatched in all of history.

# CHAPTER 5

# EVERYONE ALWAYS ACTS IN THEIR SELF-INTEREST AS THEY DEFINE IT

Self-interest is not objectionable nor reprehensible, it is just the way the world works, and it is the principal reason why government doesn't work.

We know everyone always acts in their self-interest so we must remember that when we elect them, they are not going to become non-human. People in positions of power also act in their self-interest.

That is why there is so much inertia in government, in Congress, and in the system. The special interests elect the politicians with the money and they buy influence with the agencies. It isn't a conspiracy; it's just natural, merely human nature at work. The solution is to take away the centralized power and the unfair market advantage of those who obtain the favor of government.

Self-interest is another way of saying people always act to gain a profit or a plus. People seek to avoid a minus or a loss. Arguments begin saying that religious people don't act in their self-interest because they are selfless. However, they do seek a profit or a plus, because the way they are living makes them happy through their own choice. The classic example of selflessness often cited is that of the soldier who throws his body over a live hand grenade to protect his buddies. But this is not a selfless act. This noble act of courage is the result of his choice of living out the highest ideals of courage instead of preserving his life. He gives up his life for his comrades in arms, because he gains a plus in his mind by doing so.

The North dominated the South before the Civil War. The South was trading with England, sending cotton there to be made into clothes, the clothing then returned to the South. This did not sit well with northern manufacturers and bankers. They wanted to force the South to trade with them. Therefore, in concert with Lincoln, they put a 45% tariff on English goods coming into the South. The South reacted to seek their independence.

The bloodiest, most costly and completely unnecessary war in our history resulted. Over 600,000 Americans died. What would have been so wrong with an independent South? Could they not have been friendly neighbors like Canada and the United States? There is an old axiom in economics that says: when goods don't cross borders, soldiers do.

The South should have been allowed to be independent. Maybe we could have avoided being involved in terrible wars and misadventures. The more centralized and controlled an area, the more susceptible to misadventure and mismanagement.

Was Lincoln a bad man? Probably not, but he may not deserve a monument for presiding over so many deaths. However, he was acting in his self-interest. He was obeying the wishes of the Northern manufacturers and bankers who bought and paid for him.

The key is to keep centralized power at a minimum so that when fallible people make errors, it doesn't cream all of us. You and I may make stupid unenlightened decisions but in our individual capacity, our decisions do not have the force of law.

Laws and elections do not stop people from acting in their self-interest. People are people and always will be. Everyone always acts in what they perceive to be their own self-interest. Let's make sure they don't have power over us.

# CHAPTER 6

# NOT VOTING IS A VOTE

It is widely held that you must vote in order to uphold your civic and patriotic duty. That could be true if some real change could occur as the result.

The problem is that a vote for President or Congressman or Senator is a vote that endorses our monstrous federal bureaucracy.

All we get to do is vote for the new quarterback or captain of a team that has ONE BASIC METHODOLOGY of solving problems.

Government is obsolete as a primary methodology of solving problems, and our system does not recognize this truth. The politicians debate over insignificant nuances, not important fundamental issues such as eliminating most of our counter-productive federal bureaucracy. Think of the ship of state as the Titanic with politicians scurrying around arranging deck chairs while she slips into the sea.

Oh yes, you are allowed to vote. It is a little bit like having the right to select your executioner . . . you pick the personality that you like the best.

In days gone by, the occupied villages would have a time when the farmers would bring their crops into the town square and give one-third or more to the conquering barbarians. As the conquered people presented their offering to the conquerors, they would bow down. The act of paying taxes is the same as presenting the wheat . . . when you vote, you are giving the sanction of the victim (bowing down) and saying, "Yes. I approve of your system, your methodology."

I am not suggesting that you stop paying taxes. I am suggesting that you understand that a vote is sanctioning VOLUNTARILY, the entire system.

Think of the village. You are allowed to pick the person who will flog you in the public square every April 15th.

You see, Americans are a conquered people. Our break with Great Britain was fought over miniscule taxes and regulations compared to today. Colin Powell won't bring any changes to benefit you . . . nor will almost anyone else. Dragging in an endless parade of fresh untarnished personalities only masks the completely defective machinery. It creates the illusiion of change when in reality there is no change.

The system needs radical surgery which cannot be accomplished by electing the usual cast of characters. Carefully examine the so-called Republican Revolution. It wouldn't even begin to reduce government enough. The Republicrats are arguing over how much programs should increase, not whether they should be eliminated.

The income tax should be eliminated; it was never supposed to go over 2% when passed. Government should be cut by 2/3 just for starters. You can do a much better job with your own money.

You should vote only if someone promises irrevocably to bring these kinds of MASSIVE changes. I believe there will be candidates of this type in 1996. You will find most of them in the Libertarian Party.

A basic revolution is sweeping the planet. It is the clear demonstration that government doesn't work despite its lofty objectives. Any politician or bureaucrat had better be mindful of this revolution . . . it is coming and it is inexorable. The truth will win out even though it takes a long time . . . the free market revolution is growing at breakneck speed.

Cast your vote or "not-vote" carefully.

Don't be looking down your nose at someone who does not vote. Maybe they understand better than you do that voting normally does no good and presents the sanction of the victim.

# CHAPTER 7

# ON THE WAY TO THE DANCE
# THERE WAS AN AMBUSH

Have you noticed the butterflies in your stomach? The unavoidable excitement welling-up inside you over the upcoming Presidential primaries and election? Not unless you are on the receiving end of the spoils or you are nuts or you are on drugs do you get excited about Presidential elections.

I understand that the name Dole really gets people excited that we will be helped. It's too bad former Senator Chuck Robb is not a Republican and that he and Dole cannot run for President together. The team would be Robb and Dole which is what the government does everyday. Robb and Dole are the two most accurate political names of all time.

It is very hard to get excited about politics unless you are a politician or a bureaucrat. Why is that? Could it be that no matter who gets elected, our problems stay the same? Could it be that our tax bills never go down and that things never seem to improve no matter which pretty face we elect?

In addition to a lot of other problems, there really was an ambush on the way to the dance. By that I mean, even when we elect someone to do something we believe in, they often do the opposite thing.

Here are a few examples:

Believe it or not, President Franklin Roosevelt campaigned in 1940 on the idea that "OUR BOYS WILL NEVER GO OVERSEAS TO FIGHT A WAR". 85% of the American people were against our involvement in the European war. It is now common knowledge that FDR planned for us to get into that war so those who voted according to what FDR said got just the opposite.

We voted for Lyndon Johnson because Barry Goldwater was this crazy guy who would get us into a major war in Southeast Asia. Three weeks after he was inaugurated, Johnson raised our troop level from 14,000 to 500,000 and the rest is history.

And then, there is dear old Ronnie Reagan. We elected him because he was going to bring the budget deficit under control. Har Har de Har Har. Folks, the deficit tripled under dear old Ronnie, just the opposite of what we voted for.

And don't give me the baloney of "if only we had had the right Congress". That con game will go on forever if we don't call the bluff. The fact is, we got the opposite, period.

If you get the complete opposite of what you vote for, why vote? Worse still, when you vote you are endorsing an entire system that has been established to purportedly solve problems. You endorse the entire bureaucracy.

The Presidential election and all elections for national office are nothing more than beauty contests. You are going to be flogged in the public square every April 15th. However, you are very fortunate because you get to select your flogger.

H.L. Mencken referred to an election as an "advance auction of stolen goods". Today, it is the right to select those who take your money and abuse your freedom. The bureaucracy runs the country. Congress is a tea and debating society where they wrestle with such weighty matters as whether or not to give some agency $9 billion or $10 billion. They abolish nothing. THEY TAKE NO STANDS AGAINST THE LOSS OF YOUR FREEDOM.

My definition of a presidential election is as follows: An illusory charade that makes people believe they are changing things when they basically stay the same.

For Americans to regain part of their freedom the power of the bureaucracy and its size need to be reduced by 2/3. The income tax needs to be eliminated.

Libertarian candidates want to do this so maybe there is a reason to vote. Libertarians reflect the Declaration of Independence. Check them out.

# CHAPTER 8

# MARIO CUOMO AND THE BALANCING TEST

You may say it is wrong not to help the poor. I hope you can persuade many that your cause is just. I say the greater wrong is committed if you force me and others to contribute money, because you end up impoverishing everyone to help a few. Moreover, this process is accomplished by theft and with inevitably exorbitant overhead and wastage . . .

Every time someone comes up with an argument to empower government to address some social ill, you must ask the question: at whose expense, and what are the costs on the other side of the ledger?

Former governor Mario Cuomo states that the safety net will not be there for those truly in need. He also says that taxes must be cut drastically. Money doesn't grow on trees. If the income tax were eliminated, can you imagine the flowering of programs to help the truly needy?

Cuomo has fallen into the trap of thinking that the government is the only way to address and solve problems. Most reasonable people agree that the poor and disadvantaged should be helped. The disagreements occur over the best methodology. RECOGNIZE early that you are never going to have perfection. You will always have poor, and you will always have starving people.

The key question is: what is the best methodology to help those people? The answer is the free market being allowed to work its magic. The results won't be perfect. The world is not perfect. But the results will be much better than those achieved under the statist system where they rob and impoverish us all in the process of trying to bring help. The market will be much more moral, and efficient as well.

You see, government as a methodology to solve problems is a discredited and obsolete methodology. Countries with free markets and lower taxes fare far better than centrally planned systems. All of the most prosperous nations on earth are those with the freest markets. If you don't like this reality, I am sorry. As effective as central planning sounded in the classroom, it is a total failure in real life.

The Mario Cuomos of this world will always tell you that they are truly worried about the little guy and in his case, I believe that he is. However, his solution involves the administration of bureaucracy that creates an intolerable cost.

KEEP IN MIND THAT SOME PROBLEMS WILL NEVER BE SOLVED. Keep in mind the balancing test. Do you want to erect governmental machinery to try to solve problems or is there a better way? Do not be so overwhelmed by the emotions of trying to help people that you create a bigger problem, which is what has happened to this country.

Our middle class has been eliminated and most people are struggling under the weight of the system. The balancing test dictates that we are better off with our money in our hands, to more effectively deal with problems and build a more powerful economy, to create jobs etc. And with our own money in our pockets, we can afford to be charitable.

Voluntary association to help people is a marvelous occurrence. I wish you luck in helping the unfortunate, and if you seek to persuade others to help, I wish you well. But please don't advocate force to seize my assets to further your plans. Use of force is the greater wrong. If you do your work well, I just might join in to help you help others.

It's the peaceful, moral and right way to go about your business.

# CHAPTER 9

# ON MINDING YOUR OWN BUSINESS

In the early days of America, it was a cardinal rule to mind your own business.

On Saturday, September 30th, 1995 the 16 year-old daughter of Vice-President Gore and Tipper Gore was among 12 teenagers cited by police for underage possession of alcohol at a party in Montgomery County, MD. Gore and his wife Tipper were described as upset but "dealing with it as a family and privately."

That is as it should be, but why don't they get out of my face? Have you ever noticed how there is a certain type of person that tends to want to enter politics? The mind-set is that they want to be the chosen to govern because of their power, prestige and ability to govern. These people come from a class known as busy-bodies. They love to run everybody else's lives, but usually have trouble running their own.

It is amazing how many politicians have gone bankrupt in some business before they ran for office. They run for office after having publicly demonstrated their incompetence. Have you ever looked at a political sign that said "so and so for governor" and realized what the sign really said was "so and so needs a job."

Most politicians have the best job they have ever had, and earn the most money ever as the result of being elected to office. Indeed, most bureaucrats have the best job they've ever had too. Most of them have never had a real job. The idea that there should be term limits on bureaucrats is not a bad one. Public service should be just that. But I digress.

Did you notice in your town that it was often the preacher's kid who was the wildest? The preacher was out running everyone else's lives but his kid was a mess . . . a wild-partying, free-loving, out-of-control individual.

I am not saying the Gore child did anything terribly wrong. Kids will be kids. However, Vice-President and Mrs. Gore parade around the country telling us how to live our lives. Indeed, they are part of a ruling elite that has stolen our money and intruded into the way we live in every way. Tipper Gore won an award for advancing the cause of the mentally ill, but was no more able to control alcohol abuse in her own family than the average housewife.

Like many politicians, Vice-President Gore has never held a real job. He has always lived on stolen funds. His parents were in government. The Gores are part of the ruling elite.

This elite likes us to believe that they are superhuman; they don't want us to know that their kids are normal. It's a phoney-baloney, public relations world of hiding the truth from the public. They want us to believe our leaders are infallible; they are smarter than the rest of us and that we need them to tell us how to live our lives.

Gore has spent his whole life trying to figure out how to appeal to special interests who want to seize power to dictate to the rest of us. He looks like a decent person. He has been shaped by the system built around a few people running the lives of everyone else. He might be able to compete in the real world by delivering a service or products other than brokering power for the special interests to the detriment and impoverishment of us all.

Government attracts those who can run everyone's lives but their own. The Gores should do us all a favor, get real jobs and get off our backs! Their kid may be the only honest one of the group.

# CHAPTER 10

# UNCONSTITUTIONAL VERSUS CONSTITUTIONAL

WE ALL KNOW people who are fond of saying that something is unconstitutional, if they don't like it. Unfortunately, there is almost nothing that is unconstitutional.

The constitution is a document about the powers of the central government and the only protection is afforded by the Bill of Rights to a certain extent.

The Constitution embodies the usurpation of the Declaration of Independence and the Revolution. The Declaration proclaimed the primacy of the individual and the Constitution gave powers to the government.

Despite all the protection built into it by the Founding Fathers, the Constitution has come to mean just about anything the judges want it to. If they can declare a farmer growing wheat on his own farm for consumption by his own animals to be in inter-state commerce hence subject to regulation by the federal government—which they have done—they can allow anything.

A democratic election could elect someone like Hitler. Rules could be made to incarcerate the Japanese, or fight a War in Southeast Asia, or tax half our incomes, or murder innocent children in Waco, or kill Randy Weaver's wife, or create government agencies that murder foreign leaders and sell drugs to our own people.

Friends, the Constitution doesn't protect you from very much. Our government needs to be reorganized and we must strip power from those who use their positions of authority to oppress their fellow citizens. Power corrupts and absolute power corrupts absolutely.

The Bill of Rights was added as a virtual afterthought to the Constitution (in which the word "power" is used over 40 times). When people say something is unconstitutional, they generally mean that it flies in the face of the Bill of Rights or the original Declaration of Independence. Occasionally, they mean that it has to do with going against a precedent of the court.

If you really look at what the courts have done over the years, they have steadily underwritten the centralization of governmental power. They have been the willing accomplices to the destruction of individual rights and the empowerment of the state. This was all done with the best intentions. It wasn't a conspiracy, in my opinion. People have been taught that government can solve problems. But the record shows clearly that government doesn't work; it makes problems worse, and we should try methodologies where people keep their money and their liberty.

The people need to be able to take power away from the government by asking it to butt-out of a myriad of activities where it does not belong. The national initiative process is one way of approaching this problem. We could put the elimination of certain agencies on the ballot and eliminate them if Congress refuses to act. Congress is always so concerned with its own reelection, it is unlikely to act.

The next time someone tells you that something is unconstitutional, ask them if they really are not saying that it flies in the face of the Bill of Rights and the original Declaration of Independence. Folks, you cannot rely on the system to correct itself. Jefferson said we should have a constitutional convention every 20 years. I am not sure about that but I am sure that our government needs to be radically reduced.

The best decisions are made when they are decentralized. The real issue is not whether something is unconstitutional or not, it is what makes sense in this modern age. And what makes sense is for the government to butt-out and let individuals flower. The American Revolution is the empowerment of the individual and that is at it should be.

# CHAPTER 11

# HOW DO PEOPLE GAIN VALUES?

I have often said that what government does best is manufacture valueless people. Whatever happened to the days when a person's word was his bond, when you could leave your doors open at night without fear? In those days, most people were so busy achieving the American Dream that they would not participate in the American nightmare that we have today in our crime-invested, litigated, politically-divided society.

Why was there so little crime in the early 150 years of this country's history, and what has happened to erode the value systems of so many?

First, most value systems still are not eroded. For most people, their word is their bond, and most people are not dishonest. Unfortunately, there are more bad apples than there used to be. How come?

When people are busy working to make a living, and the tax structure is not soaking up so much capital as to prevent the creation of much-needed jobs, people have a stake in the venture and tend to have higher values for two specific reasons. First of all, with money kept from the bureaucrats and put to productive use, restored prosperity means that you don't have to have both parents absent from the home just to make a living. Taxation is an assault on the family and the values it teaches.

We once treated working class families more fairly. In 1948, the personal exemption was 42% of per capita personal income, while today's personal exemption is only 11% of per capita income.

The 1948 family's total income tax bill was just 2%. Today is is roughly 30%. That is a 15 fold increase. Government's huge tax burden is driving the average family into the ground, or more precisely, into the underclass. Government is depriving our workers of a chance at the American dream.

Working mothers believe they are working to make things better for their family. They are wrong. They are working to finance the growth of a fat, corrupt, and ineffective federal government.

I don't know why no one else is pointing this out, but if you look at the national figures, you find that the amount these hard working mothers earn is equal to the huge extra tax burden piled on top of us since the '50s. Mom is not working for the family. She is working for Uncle Sam.

Second, when you earn your own way, you tend to respect the property of the other person who is earning their way. You don't rip them off, because you don't want to be ripped off. You know where money comes from—from your own individual initiative and hard work—and you understand that the government cannot give you anything it didn't first steal from someone else.

If, however, you are placed in a situation where a living is provided, either by your parents or by welfare, you tend not to value property. Teaching values sounds nice, but earning your own way is the best way to instill values and respect for others' property.

The government manufactures valueless people for several reasons. It places many in a welfare, ward of the state situation which causes resentment and lack of self respect. Since your self is your number one property, you will not respect the property of others if you do not respect yourself. The tax system of the country is based on theft, which makes it difficult to create a moral example for others. The example created is that "might makes right" and that if you have force, you can take whatever you want. Prior to the income tax of 1913, the example taught in the U.S. was one of hard work and honesty, not outright theft by taxation.

Because so much capital is ripped out of the system by taxes that there are few good jobs being created, and because the Jail Industrial Complex has imprisoned so many people for victimless drug crimes (both embittering them and creating a hardened criminal class), you end up with people who would just as soon shoot you as look at you. This is why there are more random killings than ever before. Murder has traditionally been among folks who know one another, an evil at least driven by passions we can understand. Today's slaughter is fueled by mindless brutality.

O.K. What is the solution? Recognize again, there is no perfect answer, but there is a methodology that is better than government tax and spend and subsidize and welfarize. That solution is to leave tax dollars with the people who earn them.

Let their investments create jobs to give more people a stake in the venture. Stop stealing money to give it to those who won't work, thereby creating a class of valueless people.

It is true that some people will slip through the safety net, although private charity will flourish with tax dollars back in our hands. Still, some will suffer, but fewer than when the mindless bureaucracy saps individual initiative, creating a permanent underclass maintained at a subsistence level.

Bring in the balancing test. The government has created a mess! Aren't we better-off letting the free market work? Not only does it tend to create more moral people, with the bureaucratic parasites forced to work at real jobs, there is greater prosperity for all. Even now, the poorest 10% of Americans live lives that are the envy of 90% of the world's population. Why else are our borders swamped by those clamoring to come here? Imagine the level of prosperity if the government did not steal from the economy the capital we need to put on-line the superb new technology American creative genius has devised.

Again, central planning and management of society by a ruling elite does not work. It robs everyone of money, integrity, self respect and opportunity. No central planning authority, no matter how educated, can possibly know enough to make all the right decisions at each and every level throughout our economy. In a free market economy, the people are free to cast their economic votes about how our resources should be allocated. A clear and fair-minded analysis says that government should get out of the way and let the people decide for themselves what they want.

# CHAPTER 12

# THE RULING ELITE IS DECEPTIVE AND DANGEROUS

The days of the supremacy of the ruling elite are numbered. The electronic age and demonstrations of the superiority of the free market versus central planning signal the beginning of their demise. From now on, world history will be centered on the empowerment of the individual.

The ruling elite knows this, and because of this they are very dangerous. They will seek to create crisis to maintain and expand their power, trying to make us believe that we cannot survive without them.

Has the ruling elite ever been deceptive before? Here are a few examples: You have been told that the Civil War was fought over slavery. The truth is that slavery only became a major war issue during the War. Lincoln issued the Emancipation Proclamation as a wartime measure. The real reason for the war was the overall suppression of the South by Northern politicians as best shown by the 45% tariff that was placed on Southern trade with England.

They don't tell you that in school, do they? Northern interests wanted to force the South to trade with the North. Maybe Lincoln won't look so pretty under the microscope having sent over 600,000 Americans to their deaths for money.

REMEMBER THE MAINE. The American people didn't want to get into the Spanish American War, so the U.S. government staged the sinking of the *USS Maine* in order to unite our people behind the war effort.

PEARL HARBOR:  After their lovely experience in World War I, the American people were dead set by a huge margin against the idea of getting into WWII. The U.S. had broken the Japanese code (Magic) and so the leaders at the top of our country knew that the Japanese were going to attack Pearl Harbor. Roosevelt concluded that this was okay because it would unite our people behind the War effort.

VIETNAM AND THE GULF OF TONKIN:  As a transparently feeble excuse for War, our nation was rallied around the sinking of a torpedo boat.

THE BIG RED LIE:  For years we were taught to fear Soviet power. They don't even rise to the level of Third World power under the microscope. This technique of scaring us to death was very effective to keep our tax dollars rolling in. Nothing works in the Soviet Union. Their missiles probably would have rained down on their own country. (Everyone knows of the success of the Patriot missile in Desert Storm; these were produced by private enterprise. But did you hear about the Carrier missiles? They were manufactured by the Postal Service: they didn't work and you couldn't fire them.)

THE GREAT DEPRESSION:  Government apologists and enablers of our statist nightmare implicate the free market as being responsible for The Great Depression. The truth is that the Federal Reserve with its centralized planning powers (created in 1913) *shut down the money supply by 30%* in 1929. The FED kept these severe brakes on for years, thus creating The Great Depression. Imagine the impact of such a move today. Will the ruling elite try a similar move when their power is ebbing away?

There are countless other examples of outright fabrication and misrepresentation concocted by the ruling elite, including the suppression of the real story of who killed John F. Kennedy. If it were revealed who really did the killing, the government would be exposed for just how weak they really are. They want you to believe that they are all-powerful and could immediately go after who killed Kennedy. They lied to us. Their report is hogwash.

As more and more people become aware of the fact that our rulers are just normal people, people who share all the human frailties with the rest of us, they are losing their grip over us. Incidentally, I have always been baffled by statist, socialist reasoning that says "People are imperfect so they need to be ruled and led, so lets go out and elect some of these imperfect people to rule the others." All that does is magnify the imperfection of those with the power and make the consequences worse.

These rulers are just people, but they have the guns. If they would allow all the deaths of the Civil War and Pearl Harbor, what won't they do? They may stage all sorts of crises to try to hang onto the power. You become educated, and don't let them. Never resort to force and violence. The bloodless revolution, and the empowerment of the individual is underway.

# CHAPTER 13

# THE WAR ON DRUGS IS
# THE CREATION OF THUGS

If there is anything that makes my blood boil, it's the bogus War on Drugs. Those who are ignorant of history are doomed to repeat it.

Has anyone ever heard of prohibition? The U.S. had the lowest alcohol consumption rate in the world prior to prohibition and after 13 years of vigorous law enforcement, we had the highest drinking rate.

Lesson: If you want to make a little problem big, bring in the government to try to stamp it out. The campaign for passage of prohibition was financed by money from the Mafia in Sicily. Al Capone loved it. The cost of making alcohol is cheap unless it is prohibited, which raised the prices and built profit in.

Recreational drugs are very cheap to make. The only reason there is a profit in them is because they are against the law. The big profit created by government law causes people to move into the industry. It's the only reason there are sales forces trying to hook the younger generation. The profits are huge. Every time there is a drug bust, the profit goes up and more people come into the drug trade.

In a totally controlled environment such as a prison, drug sales flourish. If the government can't control drugs in prison, how can they be controlled on the streets?

The profit is too seductive. The CIA, DEA and police forces all across the U.S. have personnel profiting from drug sales.

Nineteen workers and patients were recently discovered running a drug supermarket in a VA (government) hospital in Brooklyn, according to the *Washington Post* of September 14th, 1995. Despite our multi-billion-dollar drug war, the latest official survey shows that marijuana use by teens has doubled in the last three years. Even so, despite the huge profits in drugs and all of the people in the industry only 13 million Americans or 6.2% of the population use them.

Eighty percent of crime is related to drugs. You remove the laws against them and your crime rate drops by as much as 80%. Because of turf battles, Capone-style executions and violent crimes to get money to support habits, the War on Drugs is creating a dangerous place for us all.

It is impossible to control the drug business even if you had a policeman for every man, woman and child. The corrupt police would still sell the stuff.

Removing laws against drugs doesn't mean that you endorse their use. The plain fact is that most people don't like them. I can assure you that if they want to, they can get all they want. IT IS A LIE, IT IS SUPERSTITION AND IT IS ONE OF THE GREATEST CON GAMES OF ALL TIME TO BELIEVE THAT THE GOVERNMENT CAN CONTROL DRUGS. Even conservatives such as William F. Buckley favor their legalization.

Face it. People are going to do what they want to do whether you like it or not. That independent spirit is not a bad thing. Rebellion from central authority is good. The U.S. government is using this phoney war to destroy your liberties and supposedly guard against something that less than 10% of the population is interested in. You are paying for this so that all those politicians and bureaucrats can have jobs, you sucker.

There are laws against suicide, but if someone wants to kill himself, he will find a way to do it. Who is going to protect us from the police? Who is going to protect us from the politicians who prey on our fears in order to enslave us?

# CHAPTER 14

# THE CRIMINAL JUSTICE SYSTEM DOESN'T WORK

You have been told that the O.J. trial is not typical of the criminal justice system. Actually, it is quite typical in that the system doesn't work. The only difference is that O.J. had so much money he could fight rather than capitulate as most defendants must do.

The criminal justice system did not protect Ron and Nicole; the so called deterrent effect of the system didn't prevent their murders. To punish someone afterwards is not protection it is RETRIBUTION. The criminal justice system doesn't protect and it doesn't punish either.

What are the numbers? Of reported crimes, 10% are apprehended. Of those, 3% are convicted and about half of those are innocent and have been somehow railroaded. Does it make sense to spend millions and millions on a system that only convicts 3% of reported crimes? What about non-reported crimes?

I would rather keep my tax dollars and buy protection such as a rent-a-cop or elaborate systems at my home including very tough dogs etc. *That* is protection.

There are those who argue that the courts are too lenient and that tough courts and cops would make the system work. This is not true. You cannot have a policeman follow every man, woman and child around waiting for a crime. You have to have a few police and the police are almost never there when the crime takes place. Therefore, the system cannot work because it is impossible to apprehend the criminals.

The only reason there isn't more crime is that most people are honest. The reason you do not rob and kill your neighbor is not because of the police, it is because you don't want to. There aren't that many crooks.

However, government is busy manufacturing more.

Also, when it comes to crime, remember that 80% of crime is related to the drug laws. You get rid of drug laws, the price of drugs drops and up to 80% of crime disappears immediately. Clearly, crime pays, but not if you take the profit out of the 80% drug profit-driven portion of crime. Prosecutors are ambitious, ruthless attorneys who go after someone they feel they can convict, often without regard to the guilt of the party involved. If you only caught a few in your net, you would be inclined to jump all over someone who was unlucky enough to get caught in the 10% who are apprehended. Prosecutors live off of stolen (tax money) dollars so they come into the picture with unclean hands and a murky philosophy of might makes right.

After the spectacle of all those attorneys in the O.J. case, how could one conclude that the system is a good one? All we did was enrich a bunch of loud-mouthed attorneys at the expense of everyone, free a cold-blooded killer, and nothing could bring Ron and Nicole back.

Remember, the world is going to be an imperfect place. You should protect yourself at all times. Watch out who you get involved with and occasionally people are going to be at the wrong place like Ron.

Apply the balancing test to the criminal justice system. Are we better off with our tax dollars in our pocket to buy protection or having a monstrous police system that only convicts 3% of reported crimes. The answer does not take rocket science.

If you feel you are protected by the police, you are living in a dream world. There are alternative forms of protection that are cheaper, and that work.

I believe the Vietman War was a crime of massive proportions. The system that was erected to protect you and me did this to us. We are better off without that system.

# CHAPTER 15

# WE THE JURY

Unfortunately, the elitists who have gained control over the institutions of liberty now dominate our schools and use them to perpetuate the acceptance of the status quo. Instead of teaching our children the things they need to know to become useful and productive members of a modern democracy, they have been serving up sensitivity training, and brainwashing to produce gender equity and moral relativism. Instead of learning how to be good citizens, our little ones learn disrespect for traditional values, hatred of American culture, study dumbed-down academics to gain hyped-up bogus self-esteem. As a result, we are raising a generation of moral imbeciles and cultural orphans who have no idea how to be effective Americans.

*The power of the jury.*

For example, I do not know of a single public school in the nation which teaches its students the significance of the jury in defending our freedoms. I have yet to meet a high school senior who knew Thomas Jefferson's declaration that justice is the fundamental law of the land. Chances are that students will view jury duty as an unpleasant chore to be avoided instead of as an opportunity to protect us all by seeing to it that the Justice System delivers the product its name promises.

They don't understand that the jury was intended by our Founding Fathers to stand between government power and the people. Our youngsters do not realize that as jurors they can exercise enormous power to shape the rules we live by. No teacher explains that nothing in our Constitution, or laws or

Supreme Court decisions, requires jurors to take an oath to follow the law as the judge explains it.

The jury's fundamental job is to do justice. This means the jury
has the right and responsibility to pass judgment both on facts
and the law. If strict application of the law would produce a
guilty verdict but deny justice, the jury must disregard the law.
That is their job. Nor because of technical legal niceties must
they set an obviously guilty scum-sucking psychopath free. But
because over the years, self-interested lawyers have captured
the law, become a high priesthood of "experts" who want to
control the law, lawyers and judges are among the last people in
the world who want real people to know their full rights as
jurors.

The other group who wants people to remain ignorant of their
true rights and responsibilities is the educational bureaucracy, a
body devoted to growing the welfare/police state. Much protest
surrounds their latest move: the development of new federal
history standards to be imposed on our children. The law forbids the establishment of a national curriculum, but the new
government guidelines to what our children will learn is but the
first brick going into walling parents out of our schools.

The protest of the federal takeover of our schools has centered
on the politically correct history to be shoved down our children's throats along with the deliberate omission from the
pages of history of such dead white males as Paul Revere,
Daniel Webster, Thomas Edison, Albert Einstein, and the
Wright brothers.

Even worse however is the deliberate suppression of the history
of the development of our rights as citizens and jurors. This
nation's founders knew the government they created would
someday grow so powerful as to challenge the rights of the people it was supposed to protect. As George Washington said,
"Government . . . is a dangerous servant and a fearful master."
But the new revisionist history texts your children will study

will neither teach them this nor that the Founders wisely provided a trump card citizens can use to hold the government in check: the right to a trial by a jury of one's peers.

The Constitution guarantees not once but thrice the right for a jury of private citizens to judge the facts and law, and, implicitly, if they find the law to be unjust to refuse to convict no matter what the evidence.

For nearly two centuries after my day, every school child learned this. But, in today's schools, this doesn't happen. Ignorance is the true threat to the achievement of America's destiny. As Thomas Jefferson said, "The nation which expects to be both ignorant and free expects what never was nor ever shall be." It is time to take back our country, and we can do this if we but use the tools so wisely provided by the founders of our nation. If you want to know more about these tools, you need to know about FIJA.

# CHAPTER 16

# WHAT IS FIJA?

FIJA stands for Fully Informed Jury Association. The group known as FIJA wants every U.S. citizen to be aware of the real meaning of the word jury.

The Founding Fathers by no means did everything right, but their understanding of the importance of jury nullification is one of our most important rights that extends until today.

Simply stated, it means that when a jury is to pass on the guilt or innocence of someone accused of a crime, that jury has a right to pass judgment on the facts of the case as well as the law. In other words, the jury can decide that the law is no good and refuse to apply it.

In this way, ordinary citizens act as a fourth branch of government in keeping the excesses of government in check. And, this is how juries have always operated. The Webster's 1830 definition of jury states that it is a group of people who decide the facts and merit of the law.

Some spectacular instances of jury nullification include a string of acquittals involving the *Salem Witch Trials* and *Prohibition.* When there are numerous acquittals, the government sometimes gets the message and stops trying to apply a stupid law.

Toward the end of the 19th century, the Supreme Court made decisions that have allowed jury instructions to EXCLUDE this basic and fundamental right. That is why judges always instruct juries that they can only decide the facts. Those instructions are INCORRECT. To this day, a jury can decide they don't like a law.

Once the jury has ruled, that's it; the case is over.

As we exist in a society where government has run amuck incarcerating more people than any other nation on earth, this jury principle is very important. We are living in the Jail Industrial Complex. Until we regain some control over the insanity that has been foisted upon us, the fully informed jury is some protection against the governmental juggernaut.

I strongly urge you to learn more about FIJA. They were featured in a recent NBC Nightly News segment where the NBC legal department basically concluded that FIJA is correct . . . that a jury has this right.

If you want to learn more about your true rights as a citizen under the law, you can send a stamped envelope for a free Jury Power Information Kit to the Fully Informed Jury Association, P.O. Box 59, Helmville, MT 59843, or you may contact FIJA by telephone: Larry Dodge (406) 793–5703 or Don Doig (406) 793–5550.

The FIJA organization spends its efforts informing jurors and potential jurors of their inherent rights. This is never taught in law school. It's up to all of us to tell our friends and neighbors and to support FIJA in order to prevent the legal destruction of America.

# CHAPTER 17

# WACO AND RUBY RIDGE ARE THE TIP OF THE ICEBERG

After purloining your money through taxes, the government loves to spend your money having hearings to investigate itself at your additional expense. Then the public is supposed to think that everything is wonderful, and then the public goes to sleep beside the tiger again.

Many people relax and think that the government is doing a wonderful job of policing itself.

The problem is that the government is trampling over, harassing, and ruining countless lives and businesses everyday and you never hear about it. It takes actual murder to get some attention.

What about the agonizing slow death of liberty, freedom, entrepreneurship, individual integrity, prosperity, family life etc. due to the daily travesties of government? Ruby Ridge and Waco are not some weird departure from government as usual. They are the logical extension of "might makes right". If you do not obey all of government's rules, the logical conclusion is that you are killed or incarcerated.

If you have never faced a governmental action of regulation and enforcement, it is difficult to understand just how immoral and all-powerful government is. If the law enforcers decide to come after you with all of the resources of the United States government or a state government, you have had it unless you are rich.

Those that say you should fight for your good name in court simply do not understand how the system works. The government has unlimited resources, the individual cannot afford to fight them. That is why you hear of so many consent decrees. That is why so many poor souls have to plea bargain if the government comes after them. Our prisons are full of people who do not have the financial resources of someone like O.J. Simpson. When you don't have the money, you simply knuckle under.

There is another big misunderstanding by the public. Most people believe that you are innocent until proven guilty in the American system of jurisprudence. This is essentially true with government criminal actions. However, administrative law is another matter. If the IRS, EPA, SEC, FTC, Department of Labor or any one of numerous federal agencies charge after you, you may never get a real day in court. An administrative procedure is a hearing where the judge (hearing officer) is a former employee of the agency. You are guilty until proven innocent and the entire procedure is so costly, that the average citizen-businessman simply has to sign a decree agreeing that he did wrong, even if he did not. The alternative is to go bankrupt through legal fees.

Ruby Ridge and Waco are the tip of the iceberg. The real iceberg is the day-in and day-out ruining of the free enterprise system in the U.S. by burdensome regulators and taxes. Hearings on excesses due an injustice to the real problem which is the current system itself.

We cannot hear the cry of the individual who wants to find his place in the sun but is blotted-out by government.

Our money is taken to supposedly help us through regulation. The loss of money impoverishes us. The regulation is stealing our freedoms and THE PERFECTION ATTEMPTED BY REGU-LATION IS IMPOSSIBLE. Bad stuff is always going to happen and society is a lot better off keeping money in individuals' pockets and letting them become educated consumers. The balancing test comes down in favor of the free market. Government regulation does the greater harm.

# CHAPTER 18

# CLEAR DEFINITIONS LEAD TO CLEAR THOUGHTS

You cannot have common sense ideas unless you have clearly defined terms. Muddled definitions and concepts are one of the principal reasons for the widespread lack of common sense in our land today.

Do the terms "conservative" or "liberal" have any clear meaning to anyone? Not really. They both want to run your life in different ways, so they are really part of the same team. The liberals want to run the boardroom and the conservatives want to run the bedroom.

Most of us don't want either one of them in either place. Definitely, they are part of the same team. It is the team known as "we can run your life better than you can so we will steal your money to make it happen."

In other words, it is the central government planning team with different goals for the plan. Their machinery is exactly the same and they compete to see who will be the statist group in vogue. Conservatives and liberals are both statists. Each argues for freedom in certain areas and for control in others. BUT GUESS WHAT . . . both are always in charge of the power machinery.

This confusion is even true internationally. In October of 1995, Reuters reported as follows: "The left-leaning Democratic party emerged as Latvia's largest party, but strong support for a radical right-wing group led by a German who speaks little Latvian caused a major upset." Folks, this is more muddled thinking.

The historical definition of liberalism meant that government was reduced as our tormentor and regulator; it represented the joy of man breaking away from the bonds of the king. Talk about bastardization. Now, it means big government. Conservative means big government too.

The only useful analytical tool creates a chart that runs from zero government to total government. Conservative and liberal, right and left in current usage are both forms of governmental management. Left wing, right wing, it's the same dirty bird of central control. Going back to the sensible chart showing zero government moving up a scale to total government . . . now, you have a useful tool.

We are told that Hitler was right wing and so was Mussolini; they were fascists and the communists were left wing. This is misleading nonsense. They were all big government, central authority people on the accurate scale. They just had different P.R. firms and differences of nuance.

The same is true of Conservatives and Liberals, Democrats and Republicans today. They all embrace the same methodology of controlling you, especially if they are in power. The Republicrats rule.

What we must do is reduce drastically the power of central government authority. It is an obsolete methodology. They are clinging to it because they have the best jobs they ever had. You can run your own life and the market does a better job of solving problems than government.

With your new analytical tools, you decide how much government you want. However, let's start by cutting the federal government by at least 75% and eliminating the individual income tax and the corporate income tax. When we do, our civilization will really flower.

# CHAPTER 19

# DON'T LIMIT THEIR TERMS WITHOUT LIMITING THE TERMS OF THEIR POWER

There has been a big hue and cry for term limits from the governed who are really tired of big government failure and being trampled on.

Term limits is not a bad idea but they are like putting a bandaid over a cancer. They treat a very small symptom.

The real key is taking away the power and functions of most federal agencies. Congress is really a debating society deciding how much to give each agency every year. They never truly change or eliminate anything.

We need the initiative process at the national level to take power away from the federal government and to force the government out of our lives. If all we do is limit the terms of those who govern, it doesn't improve our lives very much.

Don't misunderstand me, I am in favor of term limits and that goes for bureaucrats too because government should be a public service not a self-service smorgasbord for the auto-delusional.

However, what is really important is roll-back of the government from our lives. Do we need the U.S. Postal Service? No, we don't and their monopoly of first class mail should be removed. The law should be changed. The initiative process is a way to do this since Congresspersons are afraid to tackle the postal service. Seven militant postal unions have a lot of money to defeat any politician statesman-like enough to go after that fat, bloated, useless, outmoded piece of garbage.

Can you think of areas where the government should butt-out? I don't know about you, but I didn't ask these people to do a number of things that they do. The initiative process gives us a chance to take back our country and get these people out of our hair by systematically asking them to vacate certain functions.

The communications revolution is continuing the empowerment of the individual as expressed in the Declaration of Independence. The days of the all-knowing ruling elite are numbered. Let the word go forth: If you are involved as a member of the ruling elite, even as a bureaucrat acting as their assistant, leave your useless job now. Stand up and be counted as someone who can recognize trends and become a useful member of society.

Productivity is there for you and you will be happy too. If you are in a phoney job you know who you are. Take a real step for mankind and help productive individuals continue the American Revolution of 1776. In other words, limit your own term and take a step toward helping us remove government controls from an area where you have expertise.

The entire world is privatizing and moving toward the free market, because each person wants to be rich. Government gets in the way of people achieving their dreams. Don't limit their terms without limiting the terms of their power.

# CHAPTER 20

# THE FATAL BLIND SPOT

You can convince yourself of almost anything. If you are a bureaucrat, you can actually convince yourself that you are performing a valuable public service, although reality frequently sets in for this often-depressed group of people.

Followers of Hitler were convinced of the righteousness of their cause. The same has been true with countless other mass-murdering politicians through the years. Recently, I attended the sentencing of an acquaintance of mine, a brilliant and innocent soul who had the misfortune of getting caught in the federal machinery. Sitting there and watching the sentencing was just like watching the pistol-killing of the lady architect in the movie *Schindler's List*.

His dignity and integrity were stripped and he was figuratively forced to walk naked and whipped before the federal judicial machinery. Everything was murdered except his actual breathing. All of the federal officials including the judge think they did a great job. They have lost all perspective just as the murderers under Hitler did.

As unlikely as it seems, O.J. Simpson may *not* have murdered Ron and Nicole. The total evidence, including his pre-Bronco suicide note indicates that he did. If he did, he has even convinced himself that he didn't do it. His mind-set went like this: (1) I did it. (2) She made me do it by making me mad. (3) Because she made me mad, it wasn't me and I didn't do it. (4) The verdict in court verifies that I didn't do it.

Bureaucrats reason in a similar fashion: (1) I really need a job with secure retirement; (2) This job is a useless piece of garbage; (3) This job provides good income with secure retirement; (4) This job is important to the country.

Zealous prosecutors and law enforcement people often lose complete sight of reality because of humankind's ability to convince themselves of anything, especially when they are well paid and there is good publicity.

Again, the only way to limit this "getting carried away by floodlights and limousines" is by limiting the power of these people.

Newt Gingrich wants to execute major drug importers. How in the world will we know whether those on trial are nothing more than opponents of his hideous federal machinery of solving problems? When people's orthodoxy and livelihood are threatened, they will come after those who threaten them. Giving the government the power to execute people is the most horrendous act imaginable.

What is to prevent these officials from convincing themselves that they have a drug dealer who really isn't one? And what business does the government have in executing people anyway? Who do we punish for Vietnam? Where are the guilty?

Well, golly gee, it is a faceless bureaucracy where NO ONE IS RESPONSIBLE. I would rather face random problems from individuals than mass-delusional organizations. It is more than a little bothersome that there are hordes of federal agents running around ruining markets and lives and these people have actually convinced themselves that what they are doing is worthwhile.

# CHAPTER 21

# IN MATTERS OF DEFENSE WHY CAN'T WE BE LIKE THE SWISS?

What is America's message to the world? Freedom: the raging success of free markets and free individuals. But we are ruled by a cabal that has left this behind. Instead of peace and trade, our so-called leaders sell violence, death and destruction as a means of solving problems. Our leaders sell "might makes right" for a profit. America, Inc. is the biggest arms and weapons dealer in the world.

From the President on up, our country is engaged in selling murder and immorality. Our government makes a profit from death in concert with weapons and munitions manufacturers. This constitutes one of the most radical departures from the American dream and the message of liberty.

And, of course, our ruling elite insists that they should have a monopoly on force; they want to disarm the rest of our country. Every person in Switzerland is armed and a member of the forces who would defend the country. When Hitler calculated the difficulty of conquering Switzerland, he estimated it would cost him one million men because the Nazi invaders would be attacked from everywhere.

France, on the other hand, had the largest standing army in Europe and the Germans went around them like they weren't even there. With everyone in the U.S. armed to protect their homes, no one could occupy our nation. We would pose a much more difficult problem than a small place like Switzerland.

What is it that gives the intellectual justification for our leaders having a monopoly on force? Is it the Civil War, Vietnam, or maybe Desert Storm? Of course, we armed Sadaam to the teeth before sending our own young men and women to become sick, injured or killed.

Violence is abhorrent. It is immoral and counterproductive. To defend yourself is a right. If the Jewish people had been armed, maybe the Holocaust could have been prevented. Our leaders are the biggest purveyors of murder and mass-destruction in the world. We should take this power from them. They don't speak for us. They only line their own pockets.

I believe that the militia movement is very healthy. I am not worried about the Texas Militia fighting an adventurous foreign war. I am worried about our leaders doing so. I trust militia around the country more than I do our leaders. Who do you trust more, the Michigan Militia or the CIA, ATF or FBI?

Militias did not perpetrate the Oklahoma City atrocity. Individuals did. There will always be nuts. Were the people sane who brought us Vietnam? As terrible as Oklahoma City was, which was worse, Vietnam or Oklahoma City?

Maybe you trust central authority. I don't. I suggest that you adopt a policy of questioning authority even though our schools and media encourage you to conform. I am pleased to see a nation where individuals are retaining arms in order to protect themselves. Throughout history, the most atrocious mass-murders have been politicians, governments and dictatorial regimes. Their killings number in millions. Individual atrocities don't amount to a fleck of dust on the scale.

We can trust the good and just people of this nation. We can not allow centralized power to continue as it is proceeding. They brought us Vietnam and Desert Storm. What evil do they plan next?

The Swiss are neutral, trade with everyone and will kick your butt if you invade them. Otherwise, they mind their own business. So should we. Just check with George Washington if you doubt it.

# CHAPTER 22

# CONCLUSION: WHAT SHOULD WE DO NOW?

First of all, we can save our wonderful country. The bloodless revolution is underway. Generation X is libertarian, despite their statist educations and the media apologists who constantly bombard their senses.

Apparently Generation X is a lot smarter than the statists realize. They cannot get great jobs, because so much capital is sucked out of the system for taxes. None of them expect to see Social Security and they won't unless it is changed. It can be changed and fixed without hurting anyone. Heads in the sand won't solve problems. Political chickens and charlatans like Gingrich won't solve the problem by taking it off the table. We don't need a bandaid on the cancer, we need radical surgery.

We can solve problems by addressing them honestly and with open minds, and together we will.

As you know, much is made about the greatness of democracy. Wait a minute, what if someone like Hitler were elected? What would you think of Democracy then?

The real secret is to give almost no power to central government. If they don't have much power, then they can't do much damage. The more complex a society, the less government and more decentralization is needed. Every large corporate manager knows that decentralized decisions are necessary given more complexity. We need to uninvite the government from doing a number of things it is doing. The initiative process at the national level is a good and peaceful way to begin to get government off our backs, rolling them back to their powers of the old days. We need to rid ourselves of the mountains of regulatory garbage. The over-regulation is all promise with no delivery including a retardation of progress and an impoverishment of us all. The American Initiative Committee (800–307–8425, 703–883–1355, 1320 Old Chain Bridge Road, Suite 220, McLean, Virginia 22101) is pushing for the right to place measures on the ballot in order to circumvent the inertia of Congress. Twenty-four states have it. Not one has been bankrupted by it.

Congress will not change without that kind of pressure. An ex-politican earns more out of office by brokering  the special privilege of the gridlock. We have to decrease the power of central government by asking them to butt-out of activities. Then, the price charged by brokers of power will drop and prosperity can be increased for all of us. Business receives subsidies that it shouldn't, so do farmers, so do welfare recipients. Everyone is at the trough and the people are the losers. Its time to end this immoral operation.

Get involved in the American Initiative Committee and two anti-IRS organizations: *Citizens for an Alternative Tax System* (CATS) 800–767–7577 and *Government by the People*  800–70 NO-IRS. I also recommend three magazines: *Media Bypass*, *Liberty*, and *Reason*. Become familiar with the Libertarian movement, it is most closely identified with the American Revolution of 1776.

For some of you the ideas you have read in the preceding pages may seem new. If so, it is an example of how we have all experienced gradualism. When the income tax was passed in 1913, the citizens were promised that it would never go over 1% or 2%. If they had been told it would be 15% or 36%, it never would have passed.

Gradually, the state grows in insidious ways. Just as the wild animal from the forest first comes to take grain. Soon, the farmer has gradually built a fence around the creature and freedom is lost. Our freedoms have eroded in such a fashion so that many of you do not recognize how much liberty you have lost.

If what you have read in this book is upsetting to you, don't worry, be happy. Our free market economy will do a good job of solving problems; we will help the poor get better and help the striving to have a clearer stake in the venture. At the end of World War II, Congress argued over how to assimilate the millions of armed forces personnel, they never did come up with a program but the economy took care of it.

For an excellent discussion of how the world can work on a free market basis without government providing every service, take a look at *The Market For Liberty,* an excellent book on this subject, by Morris and Linda Tannehill available in paperback from Laissez-Faire Books, 800–326–0996. I also recommend *Crisis Investing For The Rest Of The 90's* by Douglas Casey, published by Carol Publishing.

You really don't need a giant nanny. You can stand on your own feet and spend your money more wisely than someone else.

What can you do to improve things? First, do your best not to receive any benefit from stolen funds or tax dollars. Refuse to be part of the problem. All politics are personal, clean-up your own act first. Do not ask government to do *anything* for you or for a cause you favor. Seek other means. Do not strengthen the monster. If you are a bureaucrat, get the hell out and start living in the clean air of creativity and honesty.

If you are a bureaucrat, consider leaving the government. We need to form a Bureaucrat Rescue Mission along the lines of Alcoholic Anonymous to help these folks to go straight—get off the backs of taxpayers.

# CHAPTER 23

# JUST WHAT
# SHOULD GOVERNMENT DO?

First, let's agree that it shouldn't do very much. Jefferson said that government governs best that governs least. This was true, is true and always will be true. George Washington said that government is a fearful servant and a dangerous master.

Eliminate the income tax; start asking government to butt-out of many functions.

As to how much governance there should be and in what form, I leave that to you and objective think-tanks. It is now clearly demonstrated that government is obsolete and ineffectual as a methodology of solving problems. Indeed, it becomes the problem in trying to deal with problems. Government is not the solution, it is the problem.

There is a new book which provides an excellent explanation of what government should do. It is entitled *Why Government Doesn't Work* by Harry Browne, published by St. Martin's Press.

Whatever we allow it to do, it must be tightly controlled. When we eliminate the income tax and take the nourishment of cash flow away, let us examine together what vital functions there really are.

This work has been written out of love for the little person, out of love for the American Revolution of 1776. Americans, unite for the betterment of mankind and ourselves. It is not too late. Let us save America for ourselves, for our children, and as a beacon of hope to a world in chains. We did it before. Together, we can do it again just as we did in 1776.

LET THERE BE PEACE ON EARTH AND LET IT BEGIN WITH ME.

## ABOUT THE AUTHOR

Thomas Pain is the self-appointed and self-annointed Chairman of the Free Market Politburo. He lives with his wife, Suffering, in the United States. Pain and Suffering have one child, Hope. Pain has two grown children: Taxed and Oppressed.

BACK COVER PHOTO: Tom Pain wants you to become a moral human being by living your life without violating the boundaries of others.